Vera Wang:

Fashion Designer

Influential Asians

VERA
WANG

Fashion Designer

Richard Worth

 Enslow Publishing
101 W. 23rd Street
Suite 240
New York, NY 10011
USA
enslow.com

Published in 2017 by Enslow Publishing, LLC.
101 W. 23rd Street, Suite 240, New York, NY 10011

Library of Congress Cataloging-in-Publication Data
Names: Worth, Richard, author.
Title: Vera Wang : fashion designer / Richard Worth.
Description: New York, NY : Enslow Publishing, 2017. | "2017 | Series: Influential Asians |
  Includes bibliographical references and index.
Identifiers: LCCN 2015050578 | ISBN 9780766079038 (library bound)
Subjects: LCSH: Wang, Vera—Juvenile literature. | Asian American fashion designers—
Biography—Juvenile literature. | Women fashion designers—Biography—Juvenile litera-
ture. | Chinese Americans—Biography—Juvenile literature.
Classification: LCC TT505.W36 W67 2017 | DDC 746.9/2092—dc23
LC record available at http://lccn.loc.gov/2015050578

Printed in the United States of America

To Our Readers: We have done our best to make sure all websites in this book were
active and appropriate when we went to press. However, the author and the publisher
have no control over and assume no liability for the material available on those websites
or on any websites they may link to. Any comments or suggestions can be sent by e-mail
to customerservice@enslow.com.

Photo Credits: Cover, Bennett Raglin/Getty Images Entertainment/Getty Imaes; p. 6 Theo
Wargo/Getty Images Entertainment/Getty Images; p. 8 Ron Sachs-Pool/Getty Images;
p. 14 AFP/Getty Images; p. 15 Seth Poppel Yearbook Library; p. 18 The LIFE Picture Col-
lection/Getty Images; pp. 23, 32 Ron Galella, Ltd./WireImage/Getty Images; p. 28 Jamie
McCarthy/WireImage/Getty Images; p. 35 MISHELLA/Shutterstock.com; p. 36 Rabbani
and Solimene Photography/WireImage/Getty Images; p. 38 Jim.henderson/Wikimedia
Commons/Carlyle Hotel Madison 76 jeh.JPG/public domain; p. 40 DEA PICTURE LI-
BRARY/De Agostini/Getty Images; p. 42 Anwar Hussein/WireImage/Getty Images; p. 46
Roxanne McCann/Hulton Archive/Getty Images; p. 48 Jamie McCarthy/WireImage/Getty
Images; pp. 53, 91 ©AP Images; p. 55 Kevin Mazur/WireImage/Getty Images; p. 59 MATT
CAMPBELL/AFP/Getty Images; p. 63 Bryan Bedder/Getty Images for Swarovski; p. 65
Richard B. Levine/Newscom; p. 70 Pascal Le Segretain/Getty Images Entertainment/Getty
Images; p. 71 Ben Gabbe/Getty Images Entertainment/Getty Images; p. 75 Karl Prouse/
Catwalking/Getty Images; p. 77 Lawrence Lucier/Getty Images Entertainment/Getty Im-
ages; p. 82 Howard Earl Simmons/NY Daily News Archive via Getty Images; p. 85 Andrew
H. Walker/Getty Images Entertainment/Getty Images; p. 87 Bryan Bedder/Getty Images
Entertainment/Getty Images; p. 93 Al Messerschmidt/Getty Images Sport/Getty Images;
p. 96 Larry Busacca/Getty Images Entertainment/Getty Images; p. 99 Fernanda Calfat/
Getty Images Entertainment/Getty Images; p. 106 Jamie McCarthy/Getty Images Enter-
tainment/Getty Images; p. 111 Jennifer Graylock/Getty Images Entertainment for Delete
Blood Cancer-DKMS Americas.

Contents

Vera Wang

Chapter 1

BRAND VERA

Vera Wang is many things. She is a famous fashion designer of bridal gowns. She is an international celebrity. And she is a highly successful Asian American. But perhaps most significantly, Vera Wang is a brand. Like other classic American designers, such as Ralph Lauren and Calvin Klein, her name appears on a variety of consumer products—from bridal dresses to jewelry to cosmetics. Her brand has become the choice for a wide variety of Americans: wealthy consumers, Hollywood celebrities, the politically powerful, and middle-class customers who want to wear anything that carries her name.

In 1990, Wang opened a prestigious bridal salon offering custom-designed, one-of-a kind gowns for only those who could afford the very high prices. Soon her name became synonymous with stunning wedding gowns.

In 2006, Wang put her name on a fashionable collection of ready-to-wear clothing mass-produced for consumers and offered by Kohl's, the mid-level department store chain.

In 2011, the Vera brand of diamond engagement bands and wedding rings and a jewelry line called "Vera Wang Love" were showcased by Zales jewelry stores, making them available to millions of American brides.

Michelle Obama, in a black Vera Wang gown, poses with Chinese President Xi Jinping; his wife, Peng Liyuan; and President Barack Obama at a state dinner at the White House on September 25, 2015.

In 2012, Wang branched out, partnering with Hartmann Luggage on a new line of bags in black with lavender interior linings.

In 2013, Vera surprised the fashion world by designing wedding gowns not in traditional white, but in several colors of red. "A bride should look at everything she possibly can," Vera said, "just so she can experiment and see what makes her really feel beautiful or glamorous or classical or whatever she desires to be on that particular day."[1]

In 2015, Vera went even further designing bridal gowns that were meant to be edgier, sexier, and for a younger audience. These were accented by her own line of necklaces and pendants.

And that same year, First Lady Michelle Obama wore a black dress designed by Vera to an important dinner, as her husband, President Obama, honored the visiting Chinese President Xi Jinping at the White House.

Who is this American designer who has had her finger on the pulse of fashion for several decades? Read on to learn about Vera Wang's journey and what being Asian American means to her.

Chapter 2

A SPECIAL CHILDHOOD

During the first half of the twentieth century, China was torn apart by almost continuous conflict that took the lives of millions of Chinese people. The Chinese monarchy was overthrown, war broke out between the Chinese government and the invading Japanese, and finally the government led by Chiang Kai-shek was itself overthrown by the Communists in 1949.

Vera's parents, Cheng Ching Wang and Florence Wu, grew up amid this turmoil. Florence Wu was the daughter of General Wu Jing Biao, a powerful Chinese leader. And Florence's mother was the daughter of a Chinese nobleman. Florence was highly educated and received a bachelor of arts degree from Xi Nan University, which was unusual for a young woman in early twentieth-century China.

Cheng Ching Wang was born in Shanghai, China, and his father served as an influential minister in the Chiang Kai-shek government. Like Florence, he also attended college and later started a successful business. Both of Vera's parents grew up amid wealth and power, so when they married in 1939 it represented a union of privileged aristocrats.

But the days of the Chinese aristocracy were quickly coming to an end. The war with Japan destroyed much of China. Civil war between the government and the Communists finally led to the defeat of Chiang Kai-shek and the triumph of China's new leader, Mao Zedong. Like many other Chinese who had supported the government, Florence and Cheng Ching Wang were forced to flee China for new lives in another part of the world.

"She was forced because of the war to flee," Vera Wang explained, referring to her mother. "She took an incredible boat ride following my father to Bombay. They left everything behind. That was about 1944, and they didn't see each other for three or four years. My father did graduate work at MIT (in Boston) in chemical engineering. He's a brilliant, brilliant man. He knew he'd make no money as an engineer so he became a businessman instead. But my mother was never interested in money, just education."[1]

After Vera's parents had established themselves in the West, they began to divide their time between New York's affluent Upper East Side and Paris, the capital of France. Florence became a translator at the United Nations headquarters in New York City, while her husband began a pharmaceutical company, which became financially very successful.

Vera Wang was born in New York in 1949, into a life of wealth and privilege, just like the one her parents had enjoyed in China. Two years later, Florence gave birth to a second child, Kenneth.

Growing Up in New York and Paris

Large cities, like New York and Paris, are a study in contrasts. They are home to millions of poor, and working-class residents who live very modestly in unimpressive apartment buildings. In addition, there are a relative few residents of significant wealth. The wealthy live in beautiful apartments, shop at designer boutiques, regularly attend the theater, dine at expensive restaurants, and support great art museums.

Because Vera's parents were affluent, she grew up amid the glamour and beauty of New York and Paris. These experiences gave her an appreciation for culture and high fashion. Although Florence had a demanding job at the United Nations, she also had time to spend summers in Paris. As a child, Vera traveled to Europe with her mother on the luxury liner *Queen Mary*.

In those days, before transatlantic air travel became more common, ships like the *Queen Mary* provided the only real first-class accommodations for a trip to Europe. And passengers could experience the same luxurious surroundings that they enjoyed at home. Once in Paris,

Vera and her mother often visited the city's leading fashion boutiques.

Paris was the center of women's fashion, just as it had been for more than a century. During the nineteenth century, the House of Worth was the leader of so-called *haute couture*, or high fashion. The wealthy purchased one-of-a-kind Worth-designed gowns and dresses. Although they were wildly expensive, these designer clothes marked the women who wore them as Europe's fashion leaders. They were made especially for nobility as well as the wives and daughters of rich merchants, financiers, and industrialists.

During the twentieth century, designers like Christian Dior and Yves Saint Laurent presented their new fashions at haute couture shows every year. In addition to one-of-a-kind designs purchased by famous actresses or the wives of politicians and wealthy businessmen, these designers also created less expensive fashions for leading department stores.

As a child, Vera saw the new fashions as they were presented by sleek models in runway shows at boutiques in New York and Paris. In addition, she developed a sense of style from her mother, Florence, a tall, thin woman, who loved clothes. Her choice of clothing demonstrated Florence's distinctive personality, her appreciation for beauty, and her own ideas of what looked attractive on a woman.

In New York, Vera's parents enrolled her in the Chapin School, an exclusive and academically rigorous

As a child, Vera Wang attended the runway shows of the best designers in Paris and New York.

private school for girls. The Chapin School was founded in the nineteenth century by Maria Bowen Chapin for girls in kindergarten through high school. Entering the school in the early 1950s, Vera proved herself a good student who took her academic work very seriously and received impressive grades at Chapin. Indeed, her parents held Vera to a very high standard and expected nothing less from her.

They also enrolled her in other extracurricular activities. New York City offers some of the finest programs in dance, music, and fine arts found anywhere

Wang attended the Chapin School, one of New York City's most exclusive private schools. In the class photo above, Wang is seated in the second row, fourth from the right.

in the world. Vera studied ballet at a school founded by the gifted world-famous choreographer George Balanchine. She attended classical music and ballet performances at Lincoln Center, one of the world's best-known musical theaters. She also began to take ice-skating lessons with well-known coach Sonya Dunfield.

Passion for Figure Skating

Vera began skating at seven years old. And her love for figure skating soon became an obsession for her. She threw herself into the practice sessions and spent many hours perfecting her techniques on the ice-skating rink. "She was very willing to work hard. She had a passion and a hunger for skating," her coach said.[2] Her passion and hunger for success was a trait that remained with Vera for a lifetime.

Vera's goal was to compete in the Olympic Games—the gold standard for an amateur ice skater. In 1968, she teamed with male figure skater James Stuart. They competed in the pairs figure skating competition in 1968 and 1969, eventually finishing fifth in the US National Championships. Unfortunately, this was not good enough to become a member of the US Olympic team.

Vera was very upset at what she considered her "failure." She has called giving up skating "the major disappointment of my life." And it led to what she also called "a complete breakdown."[3] She had been pursuing this one ambition for a number of years. And now she was left without an immediate goal in her life.

American Women Gold Medal Winners, Olympic Figure Skating

Tenley Albright	1956
Carol Heiss	1960
Peggy Fleming	1968
Dorothy Hamill	1976
Kristi Yamaguchi	1992
Tara Lipinski	1998
Sara Hughes	2002

Meanwhile, Vera had decided to continue her education, attending Sarah Lawrence College outside New York City. Her freshman year began in 1968. At first she intended to become a pre-med student and eventually attend medical school. But she found many of the science courses less than exciting. Unsure of her next step, and no longer having the goal of training for the Olympics, Vera dropped out of Sarah Lawrence. She was floundering and she knew it.

Back to Paris

Vera moved to Paris, a city that had become so important to her as a child. There she began a relationship with French Olympic skating champion Patrick Pera. He won a bronze ice-skating medal in the 1968 Olympics,

Wang was a competitive figure skater but failed to qualify for the US Olympic team. She still loves the sport, however.

Famous Graduates of Sarah Lawrence College

Barbara Walters	1953	Television news anchor
Alice Walker	1965	Writer
Vera Wang	1971	Fashion Designer
Rahm Emanuel	1981	Mayor of Chicago
Ann Patchett	1985	Novelist
J. J. Abrams	1988	Director
Julianna Margulies	1989	Actress
Elisabeth Röhm	1996	Actress

and together Patrick and Vera became something of a celebrity couple in Paris.

After a year or so, however, the relationship ended and Vera returned to New York and Sarah Lawrence. After resuming her education as an art history major, Vera took her junior and senior years abroad. She returned to Paris, visiting museums and drawing pictures of the magnificent buildings for which the city is famous. She attended the Sorbonne at the University of Paris, one of Europe's oldest universities.

Vera loved the art and architecture in Paris. But she also loved the City of Lights because of the cutting-edge fashions that were being designed there. "When you're in Paris," she said, "you can't help but notice fashion. I wanted something to do with fashion. I would have done anything. I would have swept floors. I would have licked envelopes. I just wanted to be part of it."[4]

Chapter 3

ENTERING THE WORLD OF FASHION

Returning to New York City, Vera did manage to get a job in fashion—as a salesperson in the Yves Saint Laurent boutique. She had a talent for looking at women's lines and body shapes and finding just the right creation to make them look their best. While working at the boutique, Vera met Frances Patiky Stein, an editor with *Vogue*. *Vogue* is one of the world's most prestigious fashion magazines—some refer to it as the fashion bible. Stein told Vera that if she ever wanted to work in fashion magazine publishing to call her.

But before that time, Vera had approached her father about her future in fashion. She asked him to send her to a fashion design school in New York. But he refused. He wanted Vera to attend law school or business school for an advanced degree.

When Vera said she wanted to be a fashion designer, her father told her to get some experience in the fashion industry and prove herself. "He thought the chances of me making it as a designer were, like, less than zero. He said, 'Listen I paid for five years of undergraduate. How about law school or business school? Go to Yale Law.' I said nope."[1]

So she went out and found a job in fashion.

Vera reconnected with Frances Patiky Stein, who arranged for her to be hired by *Vogue*. On her first day at the new job, Vera wanted to impress her employers so she dressed as fashionably as possible; she wore a white silk Yves Saint Laur ent dress and high-heeled pumps. But her fashion editor, Polly Allen Mellen, immediately informed her that she would be expected to do totally unglamorous, gritty work and ordered her home to change into something much more informal.[2]

Her first job involved "everything from Xeroxing messenger slips to packing and unpacking for photo shoots"[3] of models, Vera recalled. She became an assistant to Baron Nicolas de Gunzburg, a member of the *Vogue* staff. "Me? Assistant to someone with a name like that. Can you imagine?" she has said.[4] Looking back, Vera sounded so surprised because she is a down-to-earth designer with little pretension.

The Years at *Vogue*

Vogue means "in style" or "in fashion," that is, "in vogue." Vera had expected to stay at *Vogue* for only a couple of years, soaking up as much as she could in the atmosphere

Legendery fashion editor Polly Mellen was Wang's boss at *Vogue*.
Working at the magazine allowed Wang to fine-tune her style.

of such a prestigious magazine. Instead, she remained at *Vogue* for sixteen years.

Over the decades, *Vogue* has been run by a series of highly gifted editors-in-chief. Among them was Diana Vreeland, who held the position from 1963 to 1971, leaving about the time Vera went to work at the magazine. Vreeland left behind her a legacy of energy, excitement, and forward-looking style that made a

Godey's Lady's Book

Before there was *Vogue*, there was *Godey's Lady's Book*. First published in 1830 by Louis A. Godey in Philadelphia, it was the magazine with the widest circulation in the 1850s. By 1860, the magazine had reached a circulation of 150,000 and called itself the "queen of monthlies." *Godey's* contained articles, poetry, and fiction by authors such as Nathaniel Hawthorne, Washington Irving, and Oliver Wendell Holmes. For forty years, the editor of the magazine was Sarah Josepha Hale, author of "Mary Had a Little Lamb."

The magazine also included the latest in women's fashions as well as a pattern in each issue for an item of clothing that a woman could sew at home. In 1840, when Queen Victoria of England married Prince Albert, she wore a white wedding dress—beginning a trend that has lasted until the present. *Godey's* celebrated her choice of white as the most fitting for any bride. The magazine also had a reporter, Mrs. Lydia H. Sigourney, who covered the activities of the royals in England. These were very popular with readers in the United States where there was no royalty.

significant imprint on the magazine and kept it at the forefront of women's fashion at a time when tastes and fashions were changing.

During Vera's years at the magazine, the editor-in-chief was Grace Mirabella, who ran *Vogue* from 1971 to 1988. Mirabella focused more on women's fashions in the workplace reflecting the growing women's movement in America and the new roles that women had been assuming in companies across the country. She also ran articles on health and fitness. In 1988, Anna Wintour became editor-in-chief, adding even more glamour, fashion, and chic to the magazine.

In her early years at *Vogue*, Vera worked for editor Polly Mellen. Vera regarded her as a friend and mentor. In turn, Mellen said that "Vera had all the ingredients of a star. You could tell that immediately."[5] She possessed a natural talent for fashion and design, which was honed and refined at *Vogue*. It was one of the best places for a young person to learn the fashion industry and to make important contacts that might come in handy later on.

By the time she was twenty-five, Vera had become a senior editor at the magazine. She worked with leading designers like Ralph Lauren and Geoffrey Beene and world-famous photographers like Richard Avedon. There were few other places where she might have gained this exposure to the women's clothing business. From each of them, Vera learned something new about design. No other learning experience could have been any richer or had greater impact on a young designer.

Her workday was long and frenetic, sometimes lasting almost twenty-four hours, especially during Runway Week, when the new fashions were introduced. This was the time when each well-known designer showed off his or her new designs, worn by slender models who paraded down runways where fashion reporters made notes and photographers snapped pictures of the latest fashions. Vera also traveled widely to Paris, Milan, Rome, and other fashion centers where she saw what they were showing for the new season.

Vera had very little personal life; she lived for her work. But she still found time to go out in the evenings and party at fashionable clubs. Only in her twenties, Vera could "burn the candle at both ends" and still keep going.

Vera Wang was dedicated, but also ambitious. One day, she hoped to replace Wintour as editor-in-chief at *Vogue*. But she wasn't the only editor with this ambition, and she realized that her chances of having this dream come true were not very great. "I'd waited a long time, and I knew I wasn't getting Anna's job," Vera recalled. "There were a bunch of us there, and we were all cruising around our late thirties and forties, and it was like, we had to get on with it."[6]

As a result, Vera asked for the job as European editor, leaving New York for Paris. But instead of working with designers and finding herself intimately involved with fashion trends, Vera's job changed. She now became the magazine's representative, spending most of her time wining and dining leaders in the fashion industry and keeping the *Vogue* name in front of them.

"It was a little grand for me as a job," Vera said. "I like the gritty parts of fashion, the design, the studio, the pictures. I'm not really a girl who likes to go out to lunch or cocktails or store openings. I felt very removed . . . it was just that I wanted to be a designer still. Very much."[7]

Vera returned to New York with a new dream. Once again, she went to her father. This time she asked him for a loan to start a new fashion boutique that focused only on tops for women. She called it "Ship to Shore." But her father wasn't interested, believing that it was not a good investment.

An Opportunity With Ralph Lauren

By 1987, as she looked around for other opportunities, Vera was offered a job by Geoffrey Beene, one of the world's leading designers. "Geoffrey was a real artist, and he wanted people around who would be fretting over a collar for a long time. That's what I loved."[8] Vera decided to leave *Vogue* to accept Beene's offer. She would move into another part of the fashion industry, designing clothes while broadening her experience and know-how.

On the verge of saying "yes," Vera was suddenly offered a much better job by Ralph Lauren—whose name and stylish clothes for men and women were world renown. It was a difficult decision for her to make because she admired Beene, but she needed the money so she could be financially independent.[9]

After many years at *Vogue,* Wang decided it was time for a career shift. She spent two years with classic American designer Ralph Lauren.

Vera worked at Ralph Lauren for two years. She designed lingerie and sportswear. As someone who exercised avidly, this fit neatly into Vera's lifestyle. "Vera was the first woman I knew who exercised," one of her colleagues said. "It was the moment when exercising was starting to be something you did in public and influencing fashion. She was the perfect person for it."[10] She also learned from Ralph Lauren how to market clothes and run a successful business—skills she would need in the years ahead. Designing fashionable clothes was only part of what made a designer famous. She also needed to know how to keep her name in front of the public.

Once when her father flew to Paris to see her, she had to turn down his dinner invitation because she was too busy. "I'm in the middle of the Place de la Concorde, and I had a military jacket on with pins, tape, and clamps (to adjust a model's outfit for a photo session). I looked like a terrorist or something, and my father said, 'Can't you just comb your hair and put a dress on and come to dinner with me?' I said no."[11] Her father did not understand why she chose this career path.

"It's a calling," she says. "Like being a musician. I mean, the hours of practice, the loneliness, the dedication. It was a very obsessive job for me."[12]

Chapter 4

TIME OF TRANSITION

"**I** was the girl who nobody thought would ever get married," Vera recalled about the year she turned forty and was working at Ralph Lauren. "I was going to be a fashion nun the rest of my life. There are generations of them, those fashion nuns, living, eating, breathing clothes."[1]

Vera had met Arthur Becker almost ten years earlier playing tennis. On their first date together, Becker and Wang met at a restaurant in New York. When he arrived at the table, Becker was stunned to see not only Vera but her entire family. The Wang family was very close, and Vera saw nothing unusual about inviting all of them to get their first look at Becker.

Nothing happened, however, although Becker and Wang continued to date intermittently. Both of them were far too busy for anything permanent. Then a few years later, Becker invited Vera on a vacation in Hawaii. It sounded very romantic, and Vera needed a break from her demanding schedule.

But she found the Hawaiian vacation disappointing. Becker spent most of the vacation golfing on some of the islands' beautiful courses, while Vera was left alone back in their room. One night at dinner, Becker offhandedly asked Vera to marry him. But she turned him down. It wasn't her idea of a romantic proposal, and anyway she was too busy with her career.

Instead, Vera went to work for Ralph Lauren. And her workday became even longer. But Becker and Vera had not forgotten each other. Finally in 1989, Becker proposed marriage again. This time the occasion was far more romantic. He had hidden an engagement ring in a piece of cake that the couple enjoyed for dessert. Although she still had doubts, Vera decided to go ahead with the wedding. After Vera said "yes," Becker joked: "Either she'd gotten smarter or I'd gotten more interesting."[2]

Her friend Anna Wintour had already told her, "You have got to get a family going here. You've been single for three decades now." So the couple set a wedding date.[3]

Finding the Right Dress

Vera worked in the world of fashion, so being married in just the right wedding dress was extremely important. But everything she saw looked exactly the same, and they did not please her taste. "There was one basic look at the time: froufrou."[4] So Vera decided to have her wedding

At the age of forty, Wang married businessman Arthur Becker. It was a union of two ambitious and successful New Yorkers.

dress custom designed. "I didn't really like it, but it was all that even I knew about bridal at the time."[5] Vera had her dress custom made at a cost of ten thousand dollars—very expensive for 1989.

Nor could she find anything appropriate for her four bridesmaids. All these dresses were designed for very young women, not more mature career women in their thirties and forties. Vera had to settle for something, but it was not what she wanted.

The wedding, which was held on June 22, 1989, included four hundred guests who assembled at the beautiful Pierre Hotel on Fifth Avenue in New York City. A twenty-five-piece orchestra entertained the guests following an interfaith ceremony—Becker is Jewish and Vera is Protestant.

Among the songs played by the orchestra was "Tomorrow," a favorite of Vera's and Arthur's.

A Married Life

Vera wanted to have children, but at the age of forty, it would prove to be difficult for her. She was even taking fertility drugs to increase her chances of becoming pregnant. At the same time, she decided to resign from Ralph Lauren. "It was a difficult decision," she said, "but I couldn't try to get pregnant and carry the workload. We were determined to be parents."[6]

But the fertility treatments were not working. Vera and her husband eventually decided to adopt two children. It was at this point that Vera's father came to her with a bold, new idea. The man who at first hadn't

The Pierre Hotel

The Pierre located on 2 East 61st Street in Manhattan is one of New York's most luxurious hotels. It was founded by Charles Pierre Casalasco, who changed his name to simply Charles Pierre. Earlier, he had worked at the Hotel Anglais in Monte Carlo, Monaco, but later journeyed to Paris where he studied with the finest chefs in the city. There he met the restaurant owner Louis Sherry, who offered him a job at Sherry's Restaurant, one of New York's best. Pierre met great financiers like J. P. Morgan and members of the wealthy Vanderbilt family.

After almost a decade at Sherry's, Pierre went to work at the Ritz-Carlton Hotel and finally opened his own restaurant just west of Fifth Avenue. In the late 1920s he joined with a group of Wall Street financial leaders to open the 714-room Pierre Hotel. At a cost of fifteen million dollars (over two hundred million dollars in current figures), the hotel had forty-one stories. The Pierre included magnificent rooms, suites, and even a few individual apartments in one of which Yves Saint Laurent lived.

supported her dreams of being a fashion designer suggested something no one could have imagined a few years earlier. He wanted her to open a bridal salon with her own designs.

I said, "What, are you joking? I don't want to do it." And he said, "Now is the right time, because you don't want to do it. You won't be so emotional." Isn't that bizarre? But that's my whole life, right there. And then he said, "Bridal." I said, "Are you kidding? I don't want

The Pierre Hotel, which overlooks Central Park, opened in 1930. Wang and Becker married there in 1989.

Becker and Wang adopted two daughters, Cecilia and Josephine. Together, the Becker family lived in a plush Park Avenue apartment on Manhattan's Upper East Side.

to do bridal . . . It's not fashion." I mean, that I should end up in bridal . . . I might as well have been doing scuba equipment.[7]

But her father was right. And he put his money where his mouth was. He followed up his proposal with a loan of several million dollars for Vera to open her first custom-designed bridal salon.

Chapter 5

THE WEDDING INDUSTRY

In 1990, Vera Wang opened her bridal shop, Vera Wang Bridal House Limited, at the Carlyle Hotel in Midtown Manhattan. Her father's investment, a whopping four million dollars, had made this new venture possible.

The time was right. The wedding industry had begun to take off about a decade earlier, and it would continue to grow for the next decades. Today weddings are a more than fifty-billion-dollar industry in the United States. And growing. The wedding industry employs approximately eight hundred thousand people.[1]

The average cost of a wedding in the United States is about $30,500. This is easily enough for a down payment

Wang opened her first shop in the luxurious Carlyle Hotel on Madison Avenue. It may have surprised many that Wang, with her impeccable fashion pedigree, was focusing on bridal fashions.

on a house in many parts of North America. Out of 2.6 million weddings annually, almost half of the couples who get married spend more than they originally thought they would for the wedding. New York City is the most expensive place to be married, averaging over seventy thousand dollars, and Utah is the least expensive, with an average wedding of approximately thirteen thousand dollars.[2]

A History of Weddings

Weddings began in early Greece and Rome. In those days, a man and a woman's father would agree on a contract for the wedding. The woman herself had no say

A Few Wedding Statistics

Average Cost of Wedding Dress: Over $1,000

Average Number of Guests: 141

Average Spent on Each Guest: $194

Most Popular Engagement Month: December

Most Popular Wedding Month: June

Most Popular Wedding Color for Bride: White

Longest Engagement Period: Brides in the Northeast, 15.5 months

Shortest Engagement Period: Brides in the South, 12 months

Average Bride's Age: 29

Average Groom's Age: 31[3]

in the decision because she was considered her father's property before marriage and her husband's property after the ceremony. This gave rise to the custom of "giving away" the bride.

Usually the bride and groom might give each other gifts, sacrifice a goat, and walk with their attendants to the groom's home, where he carried her over the threshold. This was followed by a lively party and a sumptuous feast for everyone in the wedding party.

These same traditions continued throughout the Middle Ages. A major difference, however, was the attendance of a priest who performed the wedding ceremony in a church. Guests brought cakes for a wedding celebration, and the bride and groom exchanged wedding rings. Women married as early as age twelve and men as early as fourteen. Of course, the average life expectancy was much shorter because of fatal diseases. The groom also received a dowry from the bride's father in money, land, or livestock. The larger the potential dowry, the more attractive the bride often seemed to be.

This ancient Greek pottery from the sixth century BC shows dancers and musicians performing in a wedding procession.

In colonial America, marriages continued to be arranged by the parents of the bride and groom. The father of a young man might write to the father of the girl explaining all of his son's virtues and why he would be a good husband. The couple usually obtained a marriage license before the ceremony, which was celebrated at a church. But a bride was often simply attired, generally in her best dress—blue was a popular color. But a special dress was not created especially for the wedding.

This changed with the marriage of Queen Victoria of England to Prince Albert in 1840. The queen wore a magnificent white dress. Although white had been worn by brides before—perhaps as early as the Renaissance— it was not common. Thanks to Queen Victoria, suddenly it became the fashion for the bride to be dressed in a white gown. Victoria's petite figure walking down the

Destination Weddings

During the early twenty-first century, destination weddings have become more popular. Instead of a traditional ceremony in a nearby church, the bride and groom select a fancy destination for their wedding. Then their guests are expected to travel there and join the bride and groom for a celebration. Some of these events occur in Hawaii, a Caribbean resort, or in a European hotel. These destination weddings are generally arranged by wedding planners who attend to all the specifics, such as the resort, the wedding dinner, invitations, and parties.

aisle at her wedding became an immediate icon and a standard for every other bride.

Wedding flowers had also become a popular part of the ceremony. In earlier periods, brides carried garlic and herbs to drive out any evil spirits that might be lurking. But these gradually changed into a bouquet of flowers that was held by the bride at the wedding ceremony.

The tradition of the best man may date from ancient times when a shortage of eligible women required some men to carry off their brides forcibly with the help of a close friend. After the ceremony, the best man could be found on sentry duty protecting the home of the married couple. Gradually, the role of best man became

In the second half of the twentieth century, the extravagance level of weddings rose, culminating in the wedding of England's Prince Charles to Lady Diana Spencer.

to accompany the groom and stand beside him during the wedding ceremony. He might also give a toast to the bride and groom at the banquet following their marriage.

By the late nineteenth century, weddings had become far more elaborate. A bride might hire a dressmaker to sew her gown. Bakers made cakes for the weddings, and florists supplied flowers. By the early twentieth century, large American department stores had opened bridal departments. More weddings were being catered, and families sent out engraved invitations to their guests. Photographers were often present at weddings, taking pictures that the bride and groom might keep in an album to remember their wedding day.

This changed during the Great Depression of the 1930s, when most people could not afford elaborate weddings. Brides went back to wearing their best dresses and marrying in simple, inexpensive ceremonies. Only the very wealthy could afford anything different.

Then, during the 1960s and early 1970s, weddings became more informal. Couples rejected the rituals of the past for simpler ceremonies that often occurred outside in a friend's backyard or at a tranquil setting in the woods. But this changed again in 1981, when Prince Charles, the Prince of Wales and heir to the British throne, married Princess Diana. Their glamorous wedding in Great Britain captivated millions of viewers and led to an upsurge in the bridal market that has never ended.[4]

Chapter 6

ON HER OWN

"I couldn't have picked a worse time to start my business," Vera Wang recalled. "It was four days before the Gulf War, in 1990, and right before a recession."[1] It seems the time wasn't right, after all. Still, her partner, Chet Hazzard—an old friend from *Vogue*, with broad experience in the design business— helped Vera get started. At first, she featured wedding gowns created by well-known, high-end fashion designers like Carolina Herrera. The average price of these gowns was about thirty-five hundred dollars. And Vera received some timely help from her friends at *Vogue*, which ran a very positive article about her new business. A stamp of approval in the fashion bible certainly was a start in the right direction.

Gradually, as she became established, Vera began offering something unique—her own designs. This proved to be difficult, at first. Vera and Chet Hazzard looked around for factories that could make high-quality dresses. But none existed. So they began building their own factories in Ohio and Florida. When the factories were finally completed, Vera could offer unique designs made from delicate fabrics, with the certainty that the finished products would be up to her high standards.

Although Vera's success may seem obvious to the public today, it was anything but a sure thing. As she remembers,

> When I started, I was scared. I had worked as a design director for Ralph Lauren and I saw how hard it was to get product made, shipped on time and sold. I knew the chances for success were very slim because it's more than about talent. It's also about timing. It's about reaching your customer. It's about having allure for the press. . . . It did not take off right away. I built up my business client by client.[2]

By 1994, when Vera's shop was becoming profitable and her factories were up and running, she began offering two lines of wedding dresses. None of Vera's creations were inexpensive. There were the so-called "ready-to-wear" dresses made in the factories. These sold from two thousand dollars to ten thousand dollars. That was expensive in an era when the average wedding gown sold for much less.

There were also her couture gowns, specially made designs for thirty thousand dollars and even higher. These appealed especially to well-to-do New Yorkers, film stars, and wealthy Europeans. "The customer

Wang became known for her modern, clean styles. These were a departure from traditional, excessively frilly, wedding gowns.

The Personal Touch

Actress Elisabeth Shue had selected one of Wang's less expensive, factory-made dresses. But she came to Vera's studio to have a special fitting so the dress might be altered to fit her perfectly. The fitter dove under the huge gown, moving back and forth to take final measurements as Shue stood perfectly still.

It was decided that a family veil, worn by Shue's mother and altered for the occasion, did not look just right and needed to be changed. When Shue's mother explained that the veil had to be finished for the wedding pictures on the following day, the fitter explained that that would be impossible. "She'll get it done," Wang assured, quickly calming everyone's nerves.[3] Vera's attention to detail and her dedication to customers are legendary in the industry. They are a large part of her success and her staying power.

embraced Vera's designs," Hazzard said. "She balanced fashion edginess with traditional elegance."[4]

Entering the World of Wang

Vera's shop was not for everyone, nor did she expect it to be. Customers did not just walk through the doors like they were entering a department store. Instead, they entered by appointment only. The shop's specially trained salespeople were there to help only fifty patrons at any one time. The World of Wang was not only designed to be a fashion center for the privileged, but also offered a unique shopping experience.

The shopping consultants offered patrons tasty food to eat and beverages to drink while they discussed the bride's tastes and expectations for a wedding dress. But it was not just advice for a gown that the staff offered each customer. They also provided ideas about shoes, jewelry, flowers, and hairstyles. In short, Vera's shop offered every client complete fashion services for her big wedding day.

The customers also had Vera, herself, who could advise every prospective bride with advice on what

Shopping at Wang's boutique was a departure from other bridal shops. It was Wang's underwhelming experience as a bride that fed her desire to make selecting a bridal gown a luxurious event.

Crime in Wang World

In 1994, soon after Vera opened her shop, an unforeseen crisis occurred. Two masked bandits forced their way into her two-story salon in the Carlyle Hotel. They had followed a Maryland family into the store, intending to rob them. The couple, Gerald and Edith Schaeffer, was visiting Vera's to select a wedding gown for their daughter Alisa. The robbers shot Gerald Schaeffer when he refused to give them his money. Edith had a sixty-thousand-dollar diamond ring on her finger, and the robbers demanded that she take it off and give it to them. When she couldn't get the ring off immediately, one of the bandits shot her, and then the robbers left with the ring. Fortunately, the couple recovered, and the bandits were eventually caught. But the publicity did not help Vera's business, and the couple later sued her. "That was a surreal thing, very spooky," Wang said later. She had not been in the store when the robbery occurred.[5]

would make her look best. Vera was a master, from her experience at *Vogue* and Ralph Lauren, at envisioning designs that were perfectly fitted to the shape and figure of each woman.

Not only did she offer traditional white gowns, but Vera also became the first to pioneer other colors, such as green and blue. "I was the first to really bring colors to weddings," she recalled.[6]

"I think I've been able to make a major artistic contribution to bridal by bringing a fashion sense to it," she explained. "Everyone wants to make a contribution. I'm not thinking bridal formulas but fashion. And I love clothes. They're a very wonderful outlet for creativity, to challenge yourself to create an image and change how things work."[7]

As a former bride herself, Wang understood what the modern, sophisticated bride wanted,

> Our kind of bridal salon didn't exist before. I didn't want it in midtown. I wanted a comfortable residential environment. And for the price of one retail dress you get a lot of attention plus all the accessories right there, and advice on everything, even flowers, and no consulting fee. I wanted to be exclusive by taste, not money. Small and caring.[8]

Wang's clientele numbered about seventeen hundred annually. And word of the quality of her dresses and services spread, helped along by more articles in widely read publications like *People* magazine. She was a success.

Chapter 7

DESIGNER FOR THE STARS

In the center of the ice rink, figure skater Nancy Kerrigan completed her program at the 1994 Winter Olympics in Lillehammer, Norway. The applause was deafening as the crowd showed their appreciation for her silver-medal-winning performance. But it was not only her skating that the crowd admired, it was also the costume she wore. The ethereal skating dress was silver and white with fifteen hundred rhinestones sewn into it and special illusion fabric underneath that looked like bare skin. It was a breakthrough in ice-skating fashion designed by someone who knew how to make a champion figure skater look her best: Vera Wang.

Kerrigan's magnificent costume gave Vera and her business the boost that they needed. She continued to receive recognition for her stellar bridal gowns. Millie Bratton, the editor-in-chief at *Bride's* magazine, said,

"She has broken a few rules by designing dresses that were sensual and uncomplicated, yet appropriate for a wedding."[1]

In 1995, Wang had enough money to expand her wedding line to include bridesmaids' dresses. These went on sale at a new location in a store called Maids on Madison located on Madison Avenue in New York. The store also sold dresses for flower girls. At Maids on Madison, Vera provided the same personal service available at her flagship salon. Soft colors and various lengths distinguished the dresses from many sold in other stores. Vera advised her clients that they should wear the same style as the bride to support a common look, but the colors could vary so everyone did not look the same.

Vera continued designing costumes for skaters, including Olympic champion Michelle Kwan. In addition, she began designing evening gowns and dresses for special occasions, like Hollywood award programs. She also began offering a line of accessories for women, including shoes, furs, and handbags.

Among Vera's best-known clients in the 1990s were actresses Holly Hunter and Sharon Stone. At the 1993 Oscar Awards, for example, Wang created a blond satin ball gown for Stone. And in 1994, Holly Hunter won an Oscar for her performance in the film *The Piano*, wearing one of Vera's creations. "Every high-class event I go to," Hunter said, "I call her. She understands the physics of someone who is 5'2" and 99 pounds. She

Wang's business was boosted by an unlikely design: the costumes worn by figure skater Nancy Kerrigan in the 1994 Winter Olympics.

Vera Wang's Tips for a Successful Wedding:

Give yourself time to plan your wedding.

Choose a guest-friendly site so everyone can get there.

Prep your bridesmaids and groomsmen so they know what to do.

Insist on flowers that bloom on your wedding day.

Eat something on the day of your wedding so you don't get lightheaded.

Make sure the runner on the aisle is flat so you don't trip.

Keep the ceremony short.

Consider your guests' dietary preferences and restrictions.

Choose songs that everyone loves.

Relax, be yourself, and enjoy your wedding.

Make sure your makeup, lipstick, and nail polish come nowhere near your wedding dress.

Watch the length of your dress so you don't trip on it.

Secure your veil.

Have a second pair of heels and hosiery on hand in case something breaks or tears.

Floss your teeth before the ceremony.[2]

In 1993, movie star Sharon Stone brought old Hollywood glamour to the Academy Awards red carpet in a satin Wang gown.

understands where to go to make a strong statement without overwhelming me."[3]

In 1997, as Vera unveiled a new collection of shoes for the bride, she also designed a wedding dress for Karenna Gore, daughter of the then-vice president, Al Gore. She created a wedding dress for Sharon Stone, who was married in 1998 in San Francisco. Stone had billed the event as a special Valentine's Day celebration. However, when her guests arrived, they soon discovered to their surprise that they were attending a marriage ceremony.

Wang seemed to be everywhere, and she was working continually. A hard worker, Vera also recognized that she had to keep innovating in her designs or risk falling

Work, Work, Work

Vera is a self-described workaholic who seems obsessed with her work.

I feel like I'm always on the job. I design in bed, from about 11 to 2. That's when I have creative time to myself. . . . I feel everything: the tribulations of business, the responsibility to people who depend on me to feed their families. Those things are always in my decision-making processes . . . Art and commerce are often conflicting concepts. You have to make compromises because the most cutting-edge things are not necessarily what sells. You have to find a balance; it's a very difficult thing to do.[4]

behind the rapidly changing fashion market. Women, she knew, were always looking for something new. The designer who did not provide it could find herself yesterday's sensation; and tomorrow, she might find herself completely out of the fashion business.

"If I were to say at any point that I feel really confident," Vera said, "or really in control, that would be a mistake. Because I don't . . . I think what it really is, is that I have an artistic soul. And I didn't know how to live without indulging that."[5]

Chapter 8

A WOMAN'S WORK

"Now I feel like I'm always on the job. Sometimes, my daughters have dinner here with me in the office. They leave for school at a quarter of 7 and I'm usually sleeping because when I get home at night, I work," Vera explained.[1]

Because Vera was unable to conceive any children, she and her husband Arthur adopted two Eurasian girls. Cecilia and Josephine both joined the family in the early 1990s when they were still infants. As they grew older, they also accompanied Vera in her shopping trips, learned to play golf and tennis with their parents, and eventually enrolled in the Chapin School—the very same exclusive private school that Vera had attended as a child.

But as any woman who runs a business knows, balancing work and family life is very difficult. Vera

Wang's spring 1999 collection featured a romantic pink chiffon dress and an elegant black-and-white floor-length slip dress.

has tried to be involved in her children's lives at school, participating in school activities and going to their teacher conferences. Then, as often as not, it's back to her office to work with a client who needs a wedding gown.

In 1998, Wang held her first solo fashion show in New York, featuring evening wear. The colors and prints were spectacular, winning Vera rave reviews from fashion critics. That same year she opened a large boutique at Saks Fifth Avenue's store in San Francisco, California. It featured Vera's line of wedding and bridesmaids' attire, as well as her evening gown and accessories collections.

In 2000, marking the tenth anniversary of opening her business, Vera decided to expand her New York store. At her runway show that year, she presented her custom wedding designs and evening wear as well as selections from the ready-to-wear bridal collection. Then she staged another fashion show in San Francisco at the Asian Art Museum. Preceded by a dinner honoring a new art show at the museum, Vera's models showed off her new line of jackets and knit skirts for women.

Vera had become well known as a fashion designer for the stars. In 1999, she had designed a wedding dress for former Miss America Vanessa Williams. A year later, she designed a wedding dress for Olympic figure skating star Kristi Yamaguchi. Each dress was different, reflecting the differing personalities of each client and the type of wedding that she had planned for herself.

Vera and Barbie

Barbie is one of the most popular dolls ever created, and over the years famous designers have been asked to design clothes for her. In 1998, Vera designed a Vera Wang Bride Barbie doll wearing a white satin dress, with velvet bows and a beaded back. The doll's dress had a long train and a garter belt with a blue flower in it. A year later, Vera was asked to design the clothes for another Barbie doll. This one was dressed in a long purple gown with a red sash—an evening dress designed for special star-studded occasions like the Oscar Awards.

"I always get involved in a wedding," Wang explained. "Otherwise I can't design the dress."[2]

Growing the Business

During the early part of the twenty-first century, Wang's business kept growing. The number of employees had reached two hundred, and her brand had become a worldwide phenomenon. "Intense? Without a doubt!" her husband admitted. "She is totally committed to what she's doing. And like everything, it's a blessing and a curse."[3] Fortunately, Arthur Becker seemed to understand his wife's obsession because he was also a workaholic.

Vera's business, like those of other famous designers, eventually took her into licensing. Under this arrangement, her name appeared on a product and she was involved in its design, but it was sold and marketed by another company. The company paid Vera for the use of her name.

Vera understood the need to continue to expand her business, rather than coast on her past achievements:

> There isn't room in fashion today for little businesses. Not everyone needs to be as big as Calvin Klein or Ralph Lauren. But it's a question of survival. If you can't grow as a company, you can't meet fiscal responsibilities—raises, medical coverage, expanding the business. It's grow or die, as they say on Wall Street. It's about the bottom line. Anybody who says it isn't, isn't really in business.[4]

Shoes are one of Vera's favorite fashion items, and she buys numerous pairs of them each year. In 1997, she signed a licensing arrangement with an Italian company named Rossimoda to market a line of Vera Wang shoes to accompany her gowns.

In 1999, she made an agreement with the Newmont Group for a line of leather and furs to accompany her wedding and evening gowns. These accessories included belts, pocketbooks, and fur pieces on the dresses. That same year Vera was also elected to the board of the Council of Fashion Designers of America (CFDA)—a high honor for any designer. Its members included some of the most famous fashion designers in the world.

Another licensing deal involved Unilever Cosmetics International. The giant Dutch company made an agreement to produce a line of Vera Lang perfumes. In 2001, a line of Vera Wang-designed eyeglasses appeared under a licensing arrangement with Couteur Design

Wang had learned a lot from Ralph Lauren, shown here at a CFDA awards ceremony, including the importance of expanding her brand.

Group and Kenmark Optical. And in 2001, Vera also signed a deal with china and glassmakers Waterford Wedgwood USA to produce plates, vases, and wineglasses.

Top designers are always looking for products that seem to be natural extensions of their brands. Home decoration, eyeglasses, and shoes seemed to fit perfectly with the gowns and wedding designs that Vera was creating. Indeed, during 2001, she signed another licensing deal to produce shoes—this one with the high-end manufacturer and retailer Stuart Weitzman—for shoes retailing at two hundred dollars and three hundred dollars a pair.

These licensing arrangements enabled Vera to extend her brand very effectively. Each product maintained her standards of high excellence and was marked by Vera's approach to design. "I would be lying if I said I don't like to dress supermodels or create clothing perfect for a runway," Vera explained. "But I also know that I can make any figure look the best it can."[5]

In 2001, Vera published her signature book, *Vera Wang on Weddings,* which included advice from the woman whose name had become synonymous with America's most prestigious and distinctive wedding fashion designs. In her book, Wang stresses the importance of the wedding gown,

> Whether she is schoolmarm or siren, flower child or princess, socialite or career girl, or a bit of each rolled into one, the bride should choose a gown that reflects who she is above and before all else. A wedding gown must always embody the individual.[6]

Wang signed copies of her wedding book for fans at a promotional event. There was perhaps no one better qualified to dispense advice on all things matrimonial than the queen of wedding gowns.

Wang also points out how the bride's dress is more than just clothing: "It is the embodiment of a dream... Imagine all the complexity of human emotion and expectation at the crossroads of fantasy and reality. Then add considerations of tradition, propriety, sensuality and fashion, and capture all of that in one dress. It isn't easy."[7]

Chapter 9

DESIGNS ON ICE

In 2007, fifteen-year-old Cecilia Becker interviewed her mother, Vera Wang, for *Seventeen* magazine. A large part of the interview focused on the influence of Wang's skating career upon her success in business.

"You were so devoted to figure skating in high school," Cecilia asked, "how did you stay focused?" Vera explained that "when I was your age I thought nothing of waking up at four in the morning and rushing to the rink just to have 10 minutes longer on the ice than my competitors . . . I had to sacrifice things, like a social life, to be a skater at 15."[1] Not only was Vera very competitive, but she also was dedicated to achieving success, even at the cost of the same type of social life that her peers in high school were enjoying.

"Did skating help make you successful off the ice?" Cecilia asked her mom. "For me the idea that I could always do better, learn more, learn faster, is something that came from skating. But I carried that with me for the rest of my life."[2]

Then Cecilia asked her mother, "How can I develop the kind of discipline you had for skating?" And Vera told her, "The key is falling in love with something, anything. If your heart's attached to it, then your mind will be attached to it. When you have a passion for something then you tend not only to be better at it, but you work harder at it too."[3]

Although Vera Wang's love affair with figure skating began as a child, it never disappeared, not even when she gave up her dream of becoming an Olympic champion. In 1999, *Town and Country* magazine ran a picture of Vera skating in New York's Central Park with her two daughters, Cecilia and Josephine Becker. Vera had never stopped skating, and she wanted to pass on her love for this sport to her two daughters.

In 2002, when Michelle Kwan won Olympic gold, she was wearing a skating costume designed by Vera. As Olivia Barker of *USA Today* wrote, "A former Olympic skating hopeful herself, Wang . . . revolutionized skating costumes much in the way she transformed bridal gowns. She took ice attire from the spangly get-ups that looked like they had leaped off a circus trapeze to elegant, subtle dresses that complement, rather than overwhelm, a skater's artistry."[4]

"All the brouhaha about the costumes, I think we contributed to it, I honestly do," Wang explained.

2002 Olympics

In 2002, Vera Wang wrote a series of articles for the fashion publication *Women's Wear Daily* on figure skating at the Winter Olympics that year in Salt Lake City, Utah. Although Wang liked the dress she had designed for Kwan, she also described the costume worn by Olympic contender Sarah Hughes and the pale blue dress worn by Sasha Cohen. Kwan's dress was dark purple with multicolored crystal flowers. However, Vera also did not hesitate to point out that some of the costumes she saw at the Olympics were not well designed for competitive skating because they interfered with the performance of the skaters.

"Though people like to view it as something theatrical and telegenic, it really is part of their equipment. It has to fit flawlessly. In no way can it impede their athletic performance."[5]

For Vera, skating costumes had to be designed just like wedding dresses and evening gowns. The costume had to fit the personality and the shape of the female skater. If it did not, the costume could get in the way of the skater's performance and cost her a medal. In short, the practical had to be combined with the fashionable.

In 2009, the world of figure skating recognized Vera's many contributions to the sport by inducting her into the US Figure Skating Hall of Fame. She joined many great skaters, including Peggy Fleming, Dorothy Hamill, and Kristi Yamaguchi—all world champions.

"It's a very special sport," Vera explained.[6] In an article about skating outfits, Wang talked about those from past Olympics that she especially liked. Not surprisingly, these included the neon yellow dress that she had designed for Nancy Kerrigan in the 1994 Olympic Games.

Wang also singled out a stretch-velvet dress worn by Michelle Kwan in the 1998 Olympic competition. In 2006, Japanese skater Shizuka Arakawa wore a blue costume. Wang has said Arakawa's costume was not to her personal taste because it seemed so showy. Wang favors more elegant, classic designs. That same year, Carolina Kostner, the Italian skater, wore a costume decorated with snowflakes, which Vera praised. "She has a more womanly, mature style but this outfit brings her youth and whimsy," Wang explained.[7]

In 2010, for the first time, Wang designed an ice-skating outfit for a male skater, Evan Lysacek, who won a gold medal at the Vancouver Olympic Games. She joined Lysacek on the ice during his practice session to understand how his body moved and how best to design a skating costume that wouldn't get in his way and interfere with his performance. "You wouldn't want someone to lose Olympic gold because their sleeve ripped off," Vera explained.[8]

That same year, Vera cochaired the twenty-fifth anniversary celebration of the Ice Theatre of New York. At the event, Olympic champion and skating legend Dorothy Hamill was honored for "her immense contribution to our sport. I was the lucky presenter (and

Wang attended *Vanity Fair's* Oscar Party with friend, fellow skater, and Olympic Gold Medalist Evan Lysacek in 2010.

a special secret . . . I designed her wedding dress last year)," Vera wrote in her blog.[9]

In an article for *Interview* magazine, Evan Lysacek interviewed Vera, who reviewed her contributions to figure skating costumes that year,

I started this year dressing you at the Olympics. That was a huge challenge because I'd never dressed men before . . . It's always challenging. You wonder whether you're up to the job. One minute I'm thinking of the

Wang supports many charities, including Figure Skating in Harlem, which provides educational opportunities and skating instruction to girls in underserved New York City communities.

technological aspects of your skating costumes—plural—and I wouldn't have wanted you not to have skated well because of some problem with the costume.[10]

In 2012, Vera appeared at a celebration for the Figure Skating in Harlem organization, serving more than two hundred students by providing them with educational and skating programs. That evening the organization honored Wang as a fashion designer for the greats of the skating world. "I'm thrilled to applaud Figure Skating in Harlem and the incredibly innovative work that they do," Wang said, "and the real stars of this evening, the girls themselves."[11]

Chapter 10

STRENGTHENING THE BUSINESS

In 2005, Cheng Ching Wang returned to China, almost sixty years after fleeing his country and the Communists. He was accompanied by his daughter, who was opening a bridal boutique called The Perfect Wedding in a fashionable Shanghai hotel, the Pudong Shangri-La. She also received the International Fashion Designer of the Year prize at the China Fashion Awards.

"[My father] showed me tradition, the Ming Empire, what another China was," Vera said. "I saw modern China. I expected bicycles and Mao [Zedong] suits and what I saw was a pre-Tokyo China with a hunger for western culture. It is a wonderfully exciting period. It's so fascinating."[1]

Wang went on to describe the merging of her cultures:

America brought me freedom and gave me freedom as a woman. In America we think anything is possible. The Chinese feel they have to work to deserve it. America gives you ease and nonchalance, which is what I try to do in my clothes. This is a very big deal for me emotionally. It really is my roots.[2]

Vera took a risk opening a boutique in China. She could not be sure how successful her boutique might be. But she was a risk-taker, which had been proven years earlier when she opened her own business. Then, ten years later, she spent four million dollars to produce her book on weddings in 2001.

Another risk that Vera took was going into the ready-to-wear business. Unlike custom-designed clothes for

Family Losses

Vera's mother, Florence Wu Wang, had not accompanied her to China. The woman who had inspired Vera's love of fashion died on January 17, 2004. Her death had followed a long illness. The following year, Vera lost Chet Hazzard, her partner in the business and a longtime friend. "His business acumen, instincts and selflessness have been essential in helping me to realize my lifelong dream of becoming a designer," she said.[3]

Then, in 2006, Vera's father, Cheng Ching Wang, died at age eighty-seven. He had loaned her the money necessary to open her first boutique and encouraged her to pursue her dream.

Wang's 2012 fall ready-to-wear collection featured architectural designs in addition to Wang's trademark sheer, romantic fabrics. The collection was not without its critics.

a single, guaranteed customer, a designer for ready-to-wear has no idea how many of her items might sell. That's true even if they are being shown in luxury stores, like Saks Fifth Avenue, and the designer, like Vera, has an international reputation. To help make this venture successful, in 2004, Vera had brought in Susan Sokol, an executive from Calvin Klein, to run this part of her company.

Vera's ready-to-wear line was sportier than her wedding dresses. The clothes were made to be worn over and over again by women who are looking for something distinctive and eye-catching, while still being practical.

While the venture took a large investment, Vera had learned the business end of design very well during her years at *Vogue* and at Ralph Lauren. To help finance the cost of the ready-to-wear line, Vera began licensing her name—much like Ralph Lauren and other famous designers had. Wang's licensing division was directed by Laura Lee Miller, who had worked with Vera on other licensing ventures.

There were shoes, sunglasses, and housewares—including linens and crystal glassware. In 2003, the Fragrance Foundation awarded Vera a FiFi Award for her perfume, Vera Wang Eau de Parfum. This fragrance had already become a best seller at Saks Fifth Avenue, purchased by brides to give them a distinctive scent at their weddings and on their honeymoons.

It was followed by a fragrance for men and other perfumes for younger women as well as a line of soap and skin cream.

Vera also worked with Rosy Blue, a diamond company, to produce diamond engagement rings and gold wedding bands. In 2004, a line of Vera's Silver and Gifts collection went on the market, a partnership with Syratech Corporation. These included silverware and placemats as well as fine china. This was followed by a Baby collection, including picture frames, a music box, and other items. These products helped extend Vera's line from weddings to honeymoons to the arrival of children. Each seemed to be a natural extension and complement for the other products.

Wang launched her first perfume, Vera Wang Eau de Parfum, in 2002. Several more fragrances for women and men followed its success.

And the following year, she designed the Vera Wang Suite for the Halekulani Hotel on Waikiki Beach in Hawaii. Decorated in soft colors with a Hawaiian elegance, at fifty-five hundred dollars per night, it symbolized the very high end of vacation luxury. The hotel also featured a Vera Wang Boutique with her licensed products.

These licensed products were earning her company an estimated three hundred million dollars annually by 2005. That same year, Vera won the Womenswear Designer of the Year Award, an honor reserved exclusively for the world's top fashion designers. All of these helped Wang keep her name in front of the public and earn additional revenue for her company.

Chapter 11

WANG FAMILY TREASURES

Cheng Ching Wang had been a highly successful businessman and he left a very impressive legacy at his death. Graduating in 1938 from Yenching University in China, Wang had served as a lieutenant colonel in the Chinese Nationalist Army during World War II. He had then escaped from China in 1943 by plane, flying over the Himalaya Mountains to India. From there he had gone to the United States, receiving a master's degree in chemical engineering from Massachusetts Institute of Technology. Then Wang and three of his friends from MIT founded their own company, US Summit Corporation, which worked extensively in Asia. At his death, Wang left a small fortune.

Much of Wang's wealth was in real estate. He owned a private golf course in New York State, where he could play his favorite sport whenever he wanted. Wang also loved beautiful homes, and he owned a number of them: an expensive apartment in New York City and houses in Pound Ridge, New York; Palm Beach; Southampton, Long Island; Singapore; and Shanghai.

Vera and her brother, Kenneth, had grown up in luxury. And Vera's appreciation for fine things came in large part from her father. For years, Vera and her children had enjoyed her father's magnificent estate in Southampton, Long Island. The Hamptons are a favorite vacation spot for wealthy and famous people, whose stylish homes overlook the water.

C. C. Wang's Southampton home lay on over two acres of expensive real estate, covering over six thousand square feet, with eight bedrooms and nine bathrooms. Mr. Wang and his wife, Florence, purchased the house in the 1970s, before the Hamptons became so expensive, for one million dollars. Shortly after Wang's death, Vera and her brother put the estate on the market, and it sold for $11.5 million in 2007.[1]

The Wangs also owned a beautiful home in Palm Beach, Florida—another vacation spot for well-to-do families. This was a Mediterranean-style estate that Vera's father had purchased in 1996 for $4.75 million. The mansion included five bedrooms, six bathrooms, a library, a richly appointed formal dining room and kitchen, as well as an outdoor patio with a view of the Atlantic Ocean.

Vera put the Florida home on the market in 2008, and it sold for nineteen million dollars.

For a number of years, Vera, her husband, Arthur Becker, and their two children lived in a magnificent apartment at 778 Park Avenue in New York City. Valued at thirty-five million dollars, their home had six bedrooms, five full bathrooms, and a library with wood-burning fireplaces. The apartment, located on the third floor of the building, covers a complete floor of the high-rise complex.[2]

After her father's death, Vera and Arthur decided to put this home on the market and purchase the home owned by her father at 740 Park Avenue. This co-op apartment—a property owned, not rented—was valued at $23.1 million. "It makes perfect sense to me," explained Michael Gross, author of a book on this prestigious building in Midtown Manhattan. "You don't inherit something like this—in some families, people inherit assets of that size; in other families they are arms-length transactions, whereby the buyer pays the value of the apartment."[3]

Gross wrote that C. C. Wang and his wife, Florence, had originally paid $350,000 for the apartment in 1983. "Just because you're selling to a relative," Gross added, "doesn't mean you can't make a couple of bucks."[4] Vera purchased her father's co-op from his estate in 2007.

Wang had never lost her love of parties and entertaining. And her home at 740 Park Avenue often served as a place where leading politicians and actors got together in New York. According to *Harper's Bazaar*, Vera "has an entire room dedicated solely to her T-shirt

Through savvy real estate investments, Wang has added greatly to her empire. Her homes are very important to her, both as private sanctuaries and as venues for the parties she loves to throw.

collection. The tops are all carefully organized by designer . . . 'Do you have thousands?' a reporter for the magazine asked. 'I couldn't even count the amount,'" Wang replied.[5]

Several years later, Vera decided to purchase a home in Beverly Hills, California, for $10.9 million. She had been spending more time in California because of her fashion business. A home in Beverly Hills, where many

Another Home

In 2013, Vera was reportedly looking at a fifty-million-dollar penthouse apartment in New York City. Located at 23 East 22nd Street, the apartment spreads over three levels with its own elevator to take people up and down. There are five bedrooms and a magnificent terrace that overlooks the city from every direction. Vera could have easily afforded such a home because by then her net worth had reached an estimated four hundred million dollars.[6]

Hollywood stars lived, seemed like a good way for her to be closer to her West Coast operations.

Originally built in 1967, the home has four bedrooms, a swimming pool, an inside theater, and a spa. Fountains stand at the entrance to the house, which has an open design, with one room flowing into the next. The interior was decorated in black and white, very modern, and a favorite of Vera's.

Chapter 12

THE FASHION INDUSTRY

Leading international designers like Vera Wang unveil their new fashion lines each year at Fashion Week. The first Fashion Week is held in February in New York City, followed by similar events in London, England; Milan, Italy; and Paris, France.

Previously, beginning in 1910, large department stores had held their own fashion shows. These events brought throngs of customers to their stores to see what was "in" for the year's fashion.

New York held its first Fashion Week in 1943 during World War II. Hailed as a great success, the event became a tradition, and fashion magazines such as *Vogue* and *Harper's Bazaar* ran articles and pictures describing the new fashions. Some reporters were praiseworthy, while others were frankly critical of what they saw. While some designers seemed to embody new trends in fashion, others had clearly missed the mark.

Fashion Week in New York included a number of shows at various hotels where thin, willowy models walked down runways wearing the latest in fashion from key designers. Eventually, Fashion Week was moved to a single location at Bryant Park off of Fifth Avenue—called Fashion Mile in New York. Then in 2010, the event moved to Lincoln Center. Now it takes place at various venues all over the city.

Fashion Week can make or break a designer, depending on the reviews. A designer bets all of his or her time, hard work, and a huge financial investment on

New York Fashion Week, now sponsored by Mercedes-Benz, has grown into a massive event that attracts media, celebrities, and the fashion elite from all around the globe.

one throw of the dice at Fashion Week. Designers show their new fashions at least twice a year, at a Fashion Week in February or March and again in September or October. The spring show unveils the fashions for that year's fall and winter, while the fall show reveals what's "in" for the next year's spring and summer. Fall fashions generally begin to be shown in stores by July, so they can be bought for the back-to-school selling season. Spring fashions arrive by early winter.

An especially important selling period is the holiday season that features clothing to be worn at special parties and other events. These must be in stores by late October or early November. Designers are often working long hours throughout the year to ready their clothing for each season.

Additionally, there are pre-fall shows and special shows that may include clothing to be worn in resorts or on cruises to the Caribbean or Mediterranean. Vera Wang generally displays her bridal clothing line and her ready-to-wear styles at spring, fall, and pre-fall events each year. In addition to the large Fashion Week shows, there may be more focused events for swimwear, everyday wear, or one-of-a-kind designer originals. Swimwear is often shown in warm climates in cities such as Miami, Florida, or Rio De Janeiro, Brazil. Designer shows are also held in Berlin, Germany, and Bangalore, Indonesia.

Over the past few years, the clothing displayed at Fashion Week shows has been changing. It used to be that spring shows featured warm, woolen clothing to

Every season, Wang puts all her efforts into her designs, culminating in the runway shows, where she gets to show off her hard work.

be worn for fall and winter. But since people work in warm buildings in winter and air-conditioned buildings in summer, fall and spring shows have been featuring short skirts and thin blouses that can be worn inside year-round.

Another change has been the increasing popularity of pre-collections, like pre-fall. One reason is that the Internet has given shoppers instant access to every new and developing trend in fashion. As a result, they want to see new styles far more often than twice a year.

"Pre-collections have probably been more visible for about the past five years," explained Susannah Frankel, the fashion director of *Grazia*. "The rise of fast fashion partly explains that—people know a lot more about fashion now than they used to and they want to see new things more often."[1]

Vera Wang, for example, shows at the large fall and spring shows as well as the pre-fall events. Many stores spend between one-half and three-quarters of their clothing budgets each year on these pre-events to ensure that new clothes are always available for their customers. Fashion Week and pre-events have now taken on different functions. "The show is about brand image," explains one store owner, "and the pre-collections are about keeping that momentum. These pieces need to be trans-seasonal. Our online business is 50 percent international and the climates where people live obviously make a big difference."[2]

Chapter 13

DESIGNS FOR ALL

In her traditional black leggings and designer top, Vera was working on a new design. As writer Patricia Morrisroe explained:

> Vera Wang is staring at a model dressed in nothing but a transparent piece of black tulle (sheer fabric). . . . "It needs to have more edge," she says in her distinctive nasal voice. . . . Finally, after pieces of fabric have been whisked on and off, Wang likes what she sees. "That's heaven," she says about a black silk jersey tunic that will later be matched with a sequined collar and a pair of rocker pants. . . . "I feel so much better now. I want everything to be young and modern. Sexy, but not too sexy. Rock and roll-but my way."[1]

What is Vera's way? It includes tremendous attention to detail. She tries this and that, shaping material on a model's body, adding accents here and there, and putting on jewelry, until she has a look that is quintessential

Vera. This is one of the secrets to her success, which has lasted for so many years. Other designers have come and gone, but Vera continues.

Her fashion line for 2005 was shown to rave reviews, and one well-known critic said Wang went "from being known as a designer of bridal and evening clothes to just Ms. Wang, designer."[2] Vera added, "It made all my years at *Vogue* and at Ralph, and doing bridal worthwhile. You're either in the history books or you're not. I didn't make the history books in skating, but I did here."[3]

That same year, the Council of Fashion Designers of America named Wang Womenswear Designer of the Year. And a year later, 2006, she won the André Leon Talley Lifetime Achievement Award from the Savannah College of Art and Design. Talley was for years *Vogue*'s longtime editor-at-large and is known for his impeccable taste and fashion influence.

Vera's father also died in 2006. And, as she unveiled her new collection, Vera was visibly weeping. They had been very close and this collection had been dedicated to C. C. Wang.

Into Kohl's

That same year, Vera took a step in an entirely different direction. She signed a multimillion-dollar agreement with Kohl's, the department store chain, selling mid-priced products, to show off her ready-to-wear designs. These included sportswear, pocketbooks, and jewelry. It would be called "Simply Vera."

Her studio provides a glimpse of Wang's creative process. All around her are bits of inspiration to help fuel her creativity.

Announcing the deal, Kohl's CEO Kevin Mansell said, "This is another great example of how Kohl's continues to differentiate ourselves from the marketplace." But some fashion experts feared that Vera might cheapen her brand name and alienate well-to-do women who had paid far more for her exclusive clothing. "In all honesty, we have weighed everything," she said.[4]

This was also a decision that Vera wanted to make in order to broaden the appeal of her fashion designs and make them affordable to many more women. In the past, "we have been quite elitist in terms of price points," Wang explained, and this "has troubled" her.[5] The decision to work with Kohl's also enabled her to invest even more money in ready-to-wear with the expectation that the financial risk would not be too great.

Late in 2006, Vera unveiled a new ready-to-wear collection. As *Vogue* reported, "You know a Vera jacket when you see it: the subtle sheen of the silk . . . the short, elbow-length sleeves; the blossoming volume below the

From the Runway to the Football Field

While unveiling her new collections, Vera, in a major departure, designed outfits for the cheerleaders of the NFL Philadelphia Eagles. It was a different look for Vera, but one designed to keep her name in front of the public and reach an entirely new audience.

bust; the rosette attached . . . She's a brand where other designers are collections of borrowed ideas."[6]

"You can't become obsolete," Wang said. "It's a different world we're playing in, and you have to stay relevant if you want to stay in the game."[7] In 2008, she also opened a new boutique in lower Manhattan, featuring an unusual, modern design by an award-winning architect. "Vera is just very cool," said a close friend. "She brings her humor and casual sense of style to everything she does."[8]

That style applies to high-end clothing as well as more moderately priced garments offered at Kohl's. "I'm not telling people that if they go into Kohl's and

The Philadelphia Eagles Cheerleaders debuted their new uniforms, designed by Wang. Wang's signature pieces for the cheerleaders achieved a balance of cutting edge and sporty.

buy my clothes they're going to feel great walking down an upscale Parisian street," Vera explained. "I take that back. With some pieces, you would feel great. But that's not how I'm billing it. It's all about how we dress today."[9]

Chapter 14

SCALING NEW HEIGHTS

In 2010, Chelsea Clinton—daughter of former President Bill Clinton and Secretary of State Hillary Rodham Clinton—married Marc Mezvinsky. Chelsea wore two wedding dresses at the star-studded event. At the ceremony itself she wore a magnificent white gown and veil. Later she changed into a Grecian-style gown with a black ribbon. Her bridesmaids wore lavender gowns with purple bows. All of the dresses were designed by Vera Wang—who was also a guest at the wedding. "It was an honor and a privilege to dress Chelsea on her wedding day," Vera said.[1]

Earlier that year, Wang had released her new line of clothing to great acclaim. "What's the reigning queen of artsy dressing supposed to do when fashion starts heading in a cleaned-up, spare, decidedly un-artsy

Wang attended the "China: Through The Looking Glass" Costume Institute Benefit Gala at the Metropolitan Museum of Art in 2015.

direction?" asked *Vogue*'s Nicole Phelps.[2] Well, Vera had not let down any of her many fans.

Vogue's writer described a black wool pantsuit "with a narrow, slightly elongated jacket, its shoulders trimmed with . . . corsages. Tailoring was a focus of this show, but Wang put her luxurious ultra-femme stamp on it: adding Mongolian lamb trim to the hem of a coat and cutting the sleeves off at the elbows so it can be worn with opera gloves." Summing up Wang's new line, *Vogue* concluded, "'Less is more' is not a concept that feels entirely natural for Wang, still she nailed it . . ."[3]

Better Bridal

Vera also "nailed it" with her new collection of bridal wear. In an interview with Vera, *Cincinnati Wedding* magazine asked where she received her inspiration for

Vera's Stores

Vera Wang has boutiques and shops around the world, including:

Athens, Greece	Shanghai, China	Beijing, China
Singapore	Taipei, Formosa	Istanbul, Turkey
Beverly Hills, CA	San Francisco, CA	Moscow, Russia
Sydney, Australia	Tokyo, Japan	Hong Kong, China
Seoul, South Korea	Chicago, IL	New York, NY
London, England	Toronto, Canada	
San Pedro Garza Garcia, Mexico		

such unusual wedding designs. "I have always been inspired by art," Vera explained, "all kinds and periods . . . not only from a visual point of view, but from an emotional view as well. I am very fascinated by other people's artistic impressions and that always sits first and foremost in my mind, as a creator myself."[4]

Asked about the trends reflected in her bridal wear, Wang answered,

> I always try to make a collection inventive in some way. The Spring 2010 Collection celebrates a new sense of freedom and fragility. From delicate, ethereal layers to pale hand-painted tulles and silks, this collection embraces a youthful charm, femininity and romance. Ribbons, buttons, bows and blossoms add to the overall whimsy. A wedding gown is about self-expression. Wear something that makes you feel beautiful and feels as good as it looks.[5]

Vera's inspirations come from other sources as well. Her black wedding dress designs "started because we based the collection on underwear," she explained to *Vogue.* She also takes into account the size of a wedding and its cultural traditions. "Is it 1,000 people, like an Asian wedding, or are there 30 at a restaurant downtown in New York, you know? So, that all relates into it as well. I like to constantly push myself further but it's also about the realities of a wedding."[6]

Her 2008 show, for example, reflected the Dutch portrait paintings from several centuries earlier. And another line of clothing seemed inspired by the French poet Baudelaire and nineteenth-century French fashions.

Wang is not afraid to think outside the box when designing her bridal gowns. There is a Wang gown to suit the taste of every bride.

"Wang likes her designs to tell stories," wrote one fashion journalist. "Her talent for creating visual drama has sometimes obscured her skills as a designer."[7] And Wang is not afraid to push the boundaries of fashion. At one of her shows, as described by a journalist, "a model appears in a strapless shirred wedding gown with floating crystal petals. It's over-the-moon gorgeous. It's edgy. It's fierce. And yes, it's black."[8]

Chapter 15

THE BEST OF THE BEST

Ivanka Trump, Victoria Beckham, Kim Kardashian, and Alicia Keyes are all celebrities, and each of them was married in a gown by Vera Wang, one of the world's most popular wedding designers.

In 2011, *Brides* magazine voted Vera's wedding dresses among the very best. As a writer for the magazine wrote, "The always edgy Vera Wang threw the bridal world a curve ball with her . . . collection when she sent a parade of nude and black dresses down the catwalk. True, the designer has featured black in bridal for more than a decade, but this bias-cut mermaid gown with its V-neck and open back is as daring as she's yet dared to be. We can't help but hope that this collection, which Wang calls 'both mysterious and sexy,' brings out the inner daredevil in all brides."[1] One of the featured gowns sold for almost seven thousand dollars.

As another writer put it, "It takes special imagination to make tulle and chiffon look so wonderful. She is the only designer with the talent I have seen. Her gowns all have dreamy shapes and are definitely far from conventional."[2]

These were her high-end bridal dresses. But she also designed a far less expensive bridal collection, White by Vera Wang, which garnered rave reviews. These gowns retailed for $800–$1400 and the bridesmaid dresses sold for $158–$198. "It gives me great pride to be able to bring my designs to more women through White by Vera Wang," she said. "With the addition of bridesmaid dresses and shoes, I am excited to provide an array of romantic, classic, and whimsical fashion for the entire bridal party."[3]

This might have been enough new lines for most designers. But Vera also introduced a ready-to-wear collection that caught reviewers' eyes. In *Vogue*, writer Nicole Phelps raved about the fur-lined parkas that Vera had designed for the fall 2011 line. "She preferred to pair her parkas and vests with pieces of a more delicate persuasion—chiffon dresses mostly, or chiffon tops paired with skinny wool flannel pants made feminine by swags of knife-pleated fabric hanging from either hip. Pleats were the collection's other dominant motif. Wang showed pleated dresses for day and night in a variety of styles: short and long."[4]

Affordable Fashion

Nor did Vera forget her designs for Kohl's in 2011. As one reviewer wrote, "The collection that Vera Wang designs for Kohl's, Simply Vera Vera Wang, is just as popular as her designer collection since the line reflects the designer's sophisticated design style yet offers price points that everyone can afford." Among the attractive new items was a line of handbags. "The handbags in the . . . collection offer classic silhouettes with both neutral colors and in fall's hottest hues from the runways."[5] And they sold for only ninety-nine dollars. Her line of clothing for the collection included tunics, attractive prints, and warm textures of fabrics layered one over another—all at prices that most consumers could afford.

Vera's collections for the following year were just as spectacular. "Whether it's a full Russian Red gown from Vera's main collection or a frothy delight from her White collection . . . Vera Wang manages to steal the season once again," wrote one reviewer. "Each new dress is designed for a different type of bride." These included the "Hippie Princess," the "Fashionista," the "Good Girl," and the "Modernista." "Vera's bridesmaids are also so charming and lovely. They could double as great party dresses for the bridesmaids. Strong shades of sapphire, amethyst, mulberry, charcoal and jet are spiked with touches of chocolate, black and crystal accents."[6]

One reviewer wrote, "Vera Wang is the queen bee of wedding dresses and she is not about to give that status up! She is a master with intricate folding, layering and draping . . . Vera Wang's tailoring is impeccable and her dresses will feel like a second skin."[7]

Ready-to-Wear

The same year Vera also released a new ready-to-wear line that featured more casual clothing with "slouchy shirts and cozy leggings . . . If she's not interested in living and working in constricting clothes," one reviewer wrote, "why would she expect, let alone encourage, other women to be?"[8]

For years, Vera's new fall collections had been the talk of Fashion Week held each February. And 2012 was no different. She continued to amaze the reviewers with her new ideas and her high-quality execution. Her fall fashions featured short skirts with tailored jackets and "wispy" dresses.

Vera and Arthur

For twenty-three years, Vera and Arthur Becker had been partners in marriage. Arthur also played a major role in her business. But in 2012, the couple decided to separate. According to one report, Vera and Arthur had been experiencing problems for some time. In fact, "they used to fight all the time in public, even at dinner . . . ." According to reporter Christopher Koulouris, "So popular had the label become, many assumed Vera Wang as its high profile frontwoman . . . was by now calling all the shots when in fact both she and her husband were actively involved within different aspects of the day to day running of the label."[9]

Awards From the Fashion Industry

In June 2013, Vera Wang received the Geoffrey Beene Lifetime Achievement Award from the Council of Fashion Designers Association. It was one of the most prestigious awards in the fashion industry. While the award was in recognition of past achievement, Vera was always looking ahead to the next fashion season and designing clothes that would continue to win praise from her customers.

In September 2013, she introduced her new ready-to-wear line for the following spring. "Get sporty! Athletic influences are a big thing for Spring on the New York runways, and Vera Wang is the latest designer to insert herself into the action," wrote *Vogue*.[10]

In a way, this new look reflected Wang's own day-to-day dress, which featured sporty black pants, blouses, and T-shirts. The new line featured black outfits with colorful accents. And the final dress was eye-catching. "She must've driven her patternmakers crazy with the finale dress—a collage of chiffon, mesh, and corded lace that came off as quite effortless," added *Vogue*.[11] Vera had long been known for making a difficult design look simple in execution.

Pretty in Pink

The following year, Vera unveiled her fall bridal collection, introduced in spring 2014. It featured dresses in pink. "Pink as sensual, pink as seductive, pink as dreamy, pink as sophisticated, pink as strong,

Wang was awarded the prestigious Geoffrey Beene Lifetime Achievement Award at the 2013 CFDA Fashion Awards.

Menswear

In 2013, Vera introduced a line of menswear distributed through Men's Wearhouse, a large retail chain. The focus was tuxedos that could be worn for formal occasions, especially weddings. This was an easy extension of Vera's bridal line. In addition, she also licensed her name to a line of men's cologne—reflecting her emphasis on the romance of weddings and other special events that bring men and women together. Vera also put her name on a selection of wedding bands for men, offered through jewelry stores, like Zales.

pink as cool," Vera's notes said. Journalist Jeannie Ma wrote, "Petal, rose, coral and peony, shades of pink in every degree, define the collection. Let's just say these gowns are not for the shrinking violet. It seems Wang's [approach] for fall is unapologetically bold."[12] Some of the dresses also featured large pink roses on the sides.

That fall, Vera showed the fashion industry her ready-to-wear line for spring 2015. "Vera Wang is a born tomboy who wears only black, yet she became the world's foremost wedding dressmaker,"[13] explained *Vogue*. Her spring line reflected both sides of her personality— simple yet artsy and colorfully decorated.

In the bridal line for spring, she featured more traditional white wedding dresses. She summed up the collection by saying "Lightness of Being: Delicate and Disciplined. Sensual and Seductive." It was more traditional Vera Wang, with each "crafted from the softest tulle, hand gathered and hand-draped over second-skin nude lining, with . . . lace . . . accents . . . ." But some of the seductive gowns, as Vera described them, were "slinky" and "hauntingly beautiful."[14]

Her latest collections, like those of the past, reflected the many sides of Vera Wang. She was at once haute couture and ready-to-wear, sophisticated and simple, forward-looking and influenced by the past. But she was always innovating, bringing the fashion world something new, something uniquely Vera.

Chapter 16

KEYS TO SUCCESS

Few designers have been so successful for so long as Vera Wang. Therefore, it may be worthwhile to ask the simple question "why?" What are the keys to her long run of success?

Perhaps it began with the role models presented to her by Florence and C. C. Wang, her parents. Both were transplanted from another culture to the relatively unfamiliar United States. But this did not prevent either of them from making a mark for himself or herself. Florence was a translator at the newly formed United Nations and C. C. became a very wealthy businessman. They worked hard to get there and Vera realized what they had achieved.

They also set very high standards for their children, Vera and Kenneth. And Vera quickly learned to demand a great deal from herself. It was no easy task to balance the demanding work at the Chapin School with the equally grueling regimen of training to become an Olympic figure skater. But Vera managed to do both. She had found a passion in ice-skating and threw herself completely into it. While her friends were enjoying the usual pursuits of teenagers, Vera was training.

While losing her dream of an Olympic medal may have hit her hard, Vera found a way to bounce back. And eventually she discovered another passion—in the world of fashion. Once again she threw herself into the fashion business, working long hours to prove that she had what it took to make her way to the top of *Vogue* magazine. "She was inspiring, her energy, her caring, never complaining which was really how she was brought up," explained her boss, Polly Mellen.[1]

Unfortunately, she was to be disappointed again, when someone else became editor-in-chief of *Vogue.* But Vera's dream of a career in fashion was not shattered, just redirected to a career in fashion design at Ralph Lauren. There she rounded out the experience she would need to open her own business.

It was a risky venture, but along with her passion and her hard work, Vera Wang was also a risk-taker. That's what it takes to open your own business. It also requires single-minded dedication to the point of obsession, long hours, and tremendous self-discipline.

Her years training to be a figure skater served Vera very well when she decided to venture out on her own.

The hard work and discipline Wang exhibited as a child figure skater
have served her well throughout her successful career.

So did her commitment to high standards, unparalleled quality, and constant innovation. All of these attributes are essential to success in the fast-changing world of fashion. Yesterday's designs cannot attract new customers or keep old customers from looking elsewhere for their clothes.

Vera drove herself and her staff continually to create the best of the best. And even amid all the high stress of the fashion world, she never lost her sense of humor. "I poke fun at myself and the industry," Vera explained. "If I didn't laugh, I don't think I'd be here today."[2]

Vera's willingness to take risks also came in handy later in her career as she branched out, extending the Vera Wang brand into other fashion lines that complemented her original business—ready-to-wear, table wear, perfumes and jewelry, and even menswear. Growing a business with prudent risks is the mark of a successful businessperson.

Finally, during her long career, Vera has also kept control of her business. She has not allowed it to be taken over by a large company. Nor has she permitted others to take over her designs. Those have remained hers. Vera's brand has not been cheapened or lost its meaning. It still means something unique, something that represents high quality, something that customers continue to demand.

That's Vera!

Chronology

1949—Born in New York.

1954—Attends the Chapin School.

1968–1969—Competes in pairs figure skating competitions; attends Sarah Lawrence College; moves to Paris.

1971—Graduates from Sarah Lawrence College; goes to work for *Vogue.*

1987—Leaves *Vogue* for Ralph Lauren.

1989—Marries Arthur Becker.

1990—Opens her bridal shop.

1994—Shop is profitable; designs two costumes for Olympic gold medal winner Nancy Kerrigan.

1995—Expands her line to include bridesmaids' dresses.

1997—Unveils new collection of shoes for brides.

1998—Has first solo fashion show in New York.

1999—Signs licensing agreement to market leather and fur designs.

2000—Tenth anniversary of Vera's business.

2001—Publishes her book *Wang on Weddings.*

2002—Designs costume for Olympic gold medalist Michelle Kwan.

2003—Wins a FiFi Award from the Fragrance Foundation.

2004—Line of Silver and Gifts collection goes on market; mother dies.

2005—Named "Womenswear Designer of the Year"; opens bridal boutique in China.

2006—Father dies; wins André Leon Talley Lifetime Achievement Award; signs agreement to market ready-to-wear line at Kohl's.

2009—Inducted into US Figure Skating Hall of Fame.

2010—Chelsea Clinton wears a Vera Wang gown at her wedding.

2011—"Vera Wang Love" wedding rings showcased at Zales.

2012—Partners with Hartmann Luggage on baggage line; Vera and Arthur Becker separate.

2013—Receives Geoffrey Beene Lifetime Achievement Award; introduces a line of menswear.

2015—First Lady Michelle Obama wears a gown designed by Vera.

Chapter Notes

CHAPTER 1. BRAND VERA

1. Dana Oliver, "Michelle Obama Wows in Black Vera Wang Dress at State Dinner," *The Huffington Post,* September 25, 2015, http://www.huffingtonpost.com/entry/michelle-obama-state-dinner-vera-want-dress_560.

CHAPTER 2. A SPECIAL CHILDHOOD

1. Alex Wichel, "From Aisle to Runway, Vera Wang," *New York Times Magazine,* June 19, 1994, http://www.nytimes.com/1994/06/19/magazine/from-aisle-to-runway-vera-wang.html?pagewanted=all.
2. Cynthia Sanz and Sue Miller, "Chic to Chic," *People,* July 20, 1998, vol. 50, no. 1, http://www.people.com/people/archive/article/0,,20125822,00.html.
3. Ibid.
4. Barbara Kantrowitz, Holly Peterson, and Pat Wingert, "How I Got There: Vera Wang," *Newsweek,* October 24, 2005.

CHAPTER 3. ENTERING THE WORLD OF FASHION

1. Amy Larocca, "Vera Wang's Second Honeymoon," *New York Magazine,* January 23, 2006, http://nymag.com/nymetro/news/people/features/15541/index4.html.
2. Elisa Lipsky-Karasz, "Vera Wang: Made of Honor," *Harper's Bazaar,* April 2011.
3. Cynthia Sanz and Sue Miller, "Chic to Chic," *People,* July 20, 1998, vol. 50, no. 1, http://www.people.com/people/archive/article/0,,20125822,00.html.
4. Larocca.
5. Sanz and Miller.
6. Larocca.
7. Ibid.
8. Ibid.

9. Ibid.
10. Ibid.
11. Lipsky-Karasz.
12. Ibid.

CHAPTER 4. TIME OF TRANSITION

1. Amy Larocca, "Vera Wang's Second Honeymoon," *New York Magazine,* January 23, 2006, http://nymag.com/nymetro/news/people/features/15541/index4.html.
2. Cynthia Sanz and Sue Miller, "Chic to Chic," *People,* July 20, 1998, vol. 50, no. 1, http://www.people.com/people/archive/article/0,,20125822,00.html.
3. Larocca.
4. Sanz and Miller.
5. Ibid.
6. Ibid.
7. Larocca.

CHAPTER 5. THE WEDDING INDUSTRY

1. Jessica Grose, "The $51 Billion Wedding Industry Toasts Post-DOMA Bump," *Businessweek,* June 28, 2013, http://www.bloomberg.com/bw/articles/013-06-28/the-51-billion-wedding-industry-toasts-a-post-doma-bump.
2. "Average Cost of a Wedding," 2015, http://www.weddingstats.org/average-cost-of-a-wedding.html.
3. Chris Jaeger, "Wedding Industry Statistics from the Knot," 2011, http://weddingindustrystatistics.com/bridal-industry/wedding-industry-statistics-from-the-knot.
4. Kate Miller-Wilson, "History of Western Weddings," 2015, http://weddings.lovetoknow.com/wiki/History_of_Weddings.

CHAPTER 6. ON HER OWN

1. Janet Carlson Freed, "Designer of Dreams," *Town & Country,* February 2002.

2. "How I Got There: Vera Wang," *Newsweek,* November 14, 2005.

3. Alex Wichel, "From Aisle to Runway, Vera Wang," *New York Times Magazine,* June 19, 1994, http://www.nytimes.com/1994/06/19/magazine/from-aisle-to-runway-vera-wang.html?pagewanted=all.

4. Cynthia Sanz and Sue Miller, "Chic to Chic," *People,* July 20, 1998, vol. 50, no. 1, http://www.people.com/people/archive/article/0,,20125822,00.html.

5. Wichel.

6. Shane Mitchell, "Wang's World," *Travel & Leisure,* October 2005.

7. Wichel.

8. Ibid.

CHAPTER 7. DESIGNER FOR THE STARS

1. Donna Bulseco, "Brides Revisited," *In Style,* Spring 2002.

2. "How I Got There: Vera Wang," *Newsweek,* November 14, 2005.

3. Janet Carlson Freed, "Designer of Dreams," *Town & Country,* February 2002.

4. Ibid.

5. Jane Sharp, "Vera Wang and her Glamorous Gowns," *Biography,* June 1998.

CHAPTER 8. A WOMAN'S WORK

1. Alex Wichel, "From Aisle to Runway, Vera Wang," *New York Times Magazine,* June 19, 1994, http://www.nytimes.com/1994/06/19/magazine/from-aisle-to-runway-vera-wang.html?pagewanted=all.

2. Jane Sharp, "Vera Wang and Her Glamorous Gowns," *Biography,* June 1998.

3. Ibid.

4. Ibid.

5. Ibid.

6. Vera Wang, *Vera Wang on Weddings* (New York: William Morrow, 2001), p. 20.
7. Ibid., p. 25.

CHAPTER 9. DESIGNS ON ICE

1. Cecilia Becker, "Dress for Success," *Seventeen,* November 19, 2007, http://www.seventeen.com/fashion/advice/a9119/vera-wang-sept06/.
2. Ibid.
3. Ibid.
4. Olivia Barker, "Kwan, Wang Put Couture on Ice," *USA Today,* February 11, 2002.
5. Ibid.
6. Samantha Critchell, "Wang Reviews Skating Outfits from Olympics Past," *Athens Banner Herald,* January 17, 2010.
7. Ibid.
8. Samantha Critchell, "Vera Wang Talks about Designs for Olympic Skaters," *San Jose Mercury News,* January 21, 2010, http://www.mercurynews.com/bay-area-living/ci_14224279.
9. Vera Wang, "A Night of Fashion, Friends, and Skating," *Vera Wang Blog,* October 26, 2010, http://www.verawang.com//.
10. Evan Lysacek, "Vera Wang," *Interview* magazine, December 15, 2010, http://www.interviewmagazine.com/fashion/vera-wang/.
11. Lois Elfman, "Figure Skating in Harlem Gala Hits a High Note," *New York Amsterdam News,* April 5, 2012.

CHAPTER 10. STRENGTHENING THE BUSINESS

1. "Taking China: Vera Wang's Long March," *International Herald Tribune,* November 11, 2005, http://www.chinadaily.com.cn/english/doc/2006-01/10/content_510929.htm.
2. Ibid.

3. Vera Wang, *Vera Wang on Weddings* (New York: William Morrow, 2001), p.???

CHAPTER 11. WANG FAMILY TREASURES

1. Mark David, "C.C. Wang's Southampton Estate," *Variety*, November 15, 2007, http://wariety.com/2007/dirt/real-estalker/c-c-wangs-southampton-estate-1201227101/.
2. Mark David, "Vera Wang Swapping Park Avenue Apartments," *Variety*, July 27, 2007, http://variety.com/d007/dirt/real-estalker/vera-wang-swapping-park-avenue-apartments.
3. Max Abelson, "Vera Wang Keeps 740 Park in the Family, Buys Late Father's Co-Op for $23.1 M," *New York Observer*, October 30, 2007, http://observer.com/2007/10/vera-wang-keeps-740-park-in-the-family-buys-late-fathers-coop-for-$23.1m.
4. Ibid.
5. Elisa Lipsky-Karasz, "Vera Wang: Made of Honor," *Harper's Bazaar*, April 2011.
6. "Vera Wang Net Worth," *Celebrity Net Worth*, 2014, http://www.celebritynetworth.com/richest-businessment/richest-designers/vera-wang-net-worth.

CHAPTER 12. THE FASHION INDUSTRY

1. Laureen Cochrane, "Fashion: How the Global Market Is Changing Seasonal Collections," *The Guardian*, January 1, 2013, http://www.theguardian.com/fashion/2013/jan/01/fashion-global-market-seasonal-collections.
2. Ibid.

CHAPTER 13. DESIGNS FOR ALL

1. Patricia Morrisroe, "Vera Wang's Fashion Empire," *Departures*, March 30, 2010, http://www.departures.com/fashion/style/vera-wang%E2%80%jj99s-fashion-empire.
2. Ibid.
3. Ibid.

4. "Vera Wang to Design Line Just for Kohl's," *USA Today,* August 24, 2006, http://usatoday30.usatoday.com/money/industries/retail/2006-08024-vera-wang_x.htm.

5. Ibid.

6. Nicole Phelps, "Vera Wang," *Vogue,* September 13, 2006, http://www.vogue.com/fashion-shows/spring-2007-ready-to-wear/vera-wang.

7. Morrisroe.

8. Ibid.

9. Ibid.

CHAPTER 14. SCALING NEW HEIGHTS

1. "Chelsea Clinton's Bridal Quick Change: Two Vera Wang Wedding Dresses," *Style News,* August 2, 2010, http://stylenews.peoplestylewatch.com/2010/08/02/chelsea-clintons-bridal-quick-change-two-vera-wang-wedding-dresses.

2. Nicole Phelps, "Vera Wang Fall 2010 Ready-to-Wear Collection," *Vogue,* February 15, 2010, http://www.vogue.com/fashion-shows/fall-2010-ready-to-wear/vera-wang.

3. Ibid.

4. Amy Knueven, "Vera Wang: Interview," *Cincinnati Wedding,* Summer 2009.

5. Ibid.

6. "Vera Wang Wedding Dress: Designer Talks Designing Bridal Gowns," *Huffington Post,* September 25, 2012, http://www.huffingtonpost.com/2012/09/25/vera-wang-wedding-dress_n_1913590.html.

7. Patricia Morrisroe, "Vera Wang's Fashion Empire," *Departures,* March 30, 2010, http://www.departures.com/fashion/style/vera-wang%E2%80%jj99s-fashion-empire.

8. Ibid.

CHAPTER 15. THE BEST OF THE BEST

1. "Best Wedding Dresses of 2011," *Brides.com,* http://www.brides.com/wedding-dresses-style/verawang-2000000001458946.

2. "Vera Wang's Bridal Spring 2011 Collection," *Wedding Dresses Style,* http://www.weddingdressesstyle.com/vera-wang-bridal-spring-2011-collection/.

3. "Every Bride Deserves to Have Great Design," *XO, Vera,* July 28, 2011, http://xovera.verawang.com/newsletters/70.

4. Nicole Phelps, "Vera Wang Fall 2011 Ready-to-Wear Collection," *Vogue,* February 14, 2011, http://www.vogue.com/fashion-shows/fall-2011-ready-to-wear/vera-wang.

5. "Simply Vera Vera Wang for Kohl's Fall 2011 Handbags Will Launch in September," *Examiner,* August 10, 2011, http://www.examiner.com/article/simply-vera-vera-wang-for-kohl-s-fall-2011-handbags-will-launch-in-september.

6. Juli Alvarez, "White by Vera Wang," *Colin Cowie Wedding.com,* June 5, 2012, http://www.colincowieweddings.com/wedding-dresses/white-by-vera-wang-fall-2012.

7. "Vera Wang Fall 2012 Bridal Collection," *Stylisheve.com,* http://www.stylisheve.com/vera-wang-fall-2012-bridal-collection/.

8. Emily Holt, "Vera Wang Fall 2012," *Vogue,* February 14, 2012, http://www.vogue.com/fashion-week-review-/862782vera-wang-fall-2012/.

9. Christopher Koulouris, "Vera Wang to Divorce Husband. He Didn't Like Being Called 'Mr. Vera Wang,'" July 12, 2012, http://scallywagandvagabond.com/2012/07/veraj-wang-to-divorce-husband-he-didnt-like-being-called-mr-wang.

10. Nicole Phelps, "Vera Wang Spring 2014 Ready-to-Wear Collection," *Vogue,* September 9, 2013, http://www.vogue.com/fashion-shows/spring-2014-ready-to-wear/vera-wang.

11. Ibid.

12. Jeannie Ma, "Vera Wang Fall 2014 Wedding Dresses," *The Knot,* https://www.theknot.com/content/vera-wang-fall-2014-wedding-dresses.
13. Nicole Phelps, "Vera Wang 2015 Ready-to-Wear Collection," *Vogue,* September 9, 2014, http://www.vogue.com/fashion-shows/spring-2015-ready-to-wear/vera-wang.
14. Andrea Cheng, "Vera Wang Returns to White Bridal Dresses for Spring 2015," *In Style,* April 17, 2014, http://www.instyle.com/fashion/vera-wang-spring-2015-bridal-collection.

CHAPTER 16. KEYS TO SUCCESS

1. Elisa Lipsky-Karasz, "Vera Wang: Made of Honor," *Harper's Bazaar,* April 2011.
2. Ibid.

Glossary

boutique—A small store, especially catering to women.

brand—A type of product created by a particular manufacturer or designer under a particular name.

chiffon—A light, airy fabric.

collection—A number of items that are similar; in fashion: a line of clothing released at the same time.

custom made—Describes a one-of-a-kind garment that is usually expensive.

Fashion Week—The week when designers unveil their new fashions.

haute couture—High style or high culture.

investment—The act of putting money towards something that has the potential to make a profit.

licensing—Formal permission given by the government or other agency to carry on some business or profession.

ready-to-wear—Describes less expensive garments produced in great quantity.

runway show—A fashion show in which models walk down a runway.

traditional—Customary.

tulle—A sheer, lightweight fabric.

vogue—In fashion.

Further Reading

Books

Bowles, Hamish and Vera Wang. *Vogue Weddings: Brides, Dresses, Designers.* New York: Condé Nast, 2012.

Dakers, Diane. *Vera Wang: A Passion for Bridal and Lifestyle Design.* New York: Crabtree Publishing, 2011.

Gallegos, Kenneth. *Vera Wang: 80 Success Facts.* New York: Enereo Publishing, 2012.

Thompson, Eleanor. *The Wedding Dress: The 50 Designers That Changed the Course of History.* New York: Prestel, 2014.

Websites

Vera Wang

www.verawang.com

This is the official website of Vera Wang.

Vera Wang—Biography.com

www.biographycom/people/vera-wang

A comprehensive website providing biographical information about Wang.

Index